DISCOVERING
ANCIENT
EGYPT

EXPLORING ANCIENT CIVILIZATIONS

DISCOVERING ANCIENT EGYPT

ERIN STALEY

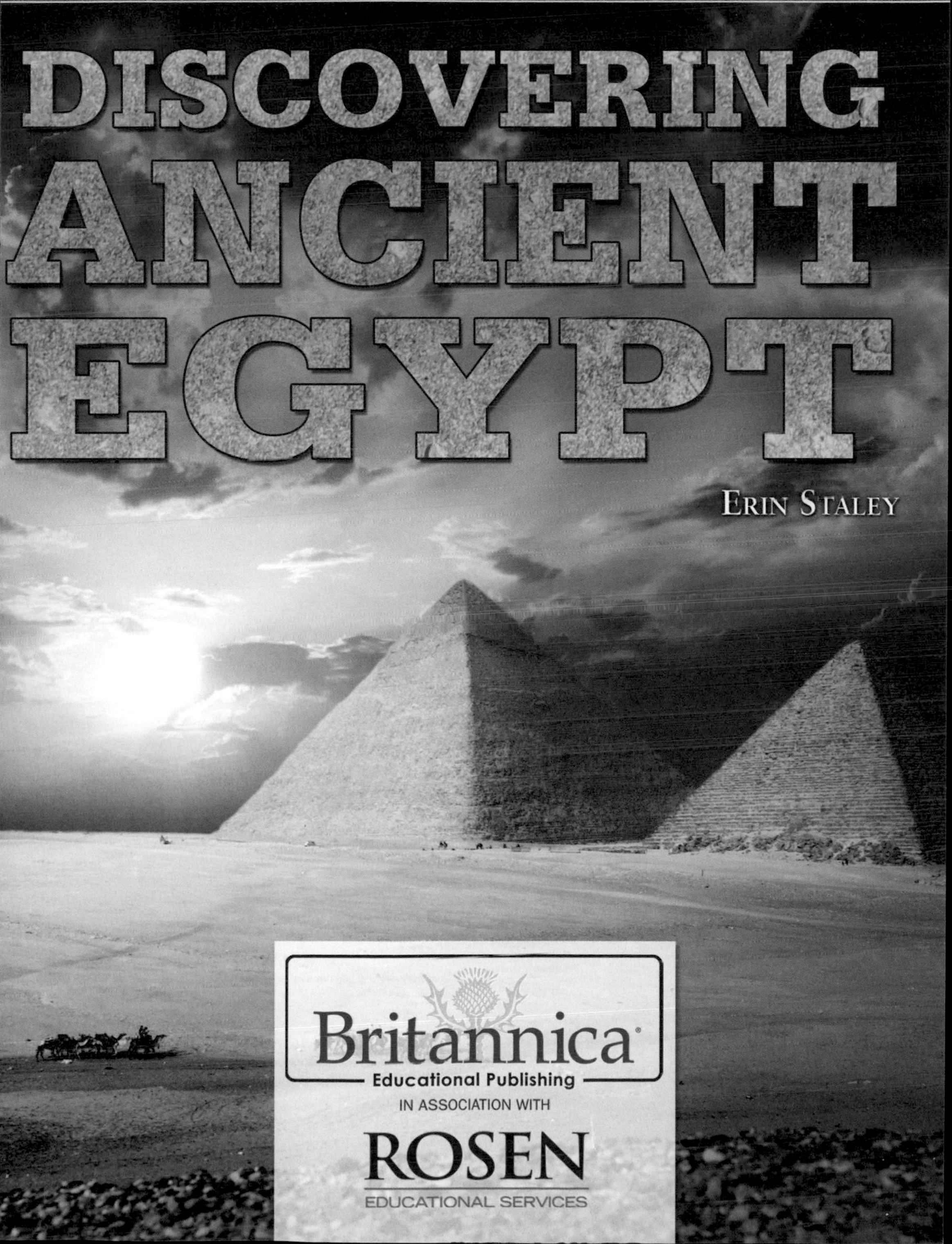

Britannica®
Educational Publishing
IN ASSOCIATION WITH
ROSEN
EDUCATIONAL SERVICES

Published in 2015 by Britannica Educational Publishing (a trademark of Encyclopædia Britannica, Inc.) in association with The Rosen Publishing Group, Inc.
29 East 21st Street, New York, NY 10010

Distributed exclusively by Rosen Publishing.
To see additional Britannica Educational Publishing titles, go to http://wwww.rosenpublishing.com.

First Edition

Britannica Educational Publishing
J. E. Luebering: Director, Core Reference Group
Anthony L. Green: Editor, Compton's by Britannica

Rosen Publishing
Hope Lourie Killcoyne: Executive Editor
Jacob R. Steinberg: Editor
Nelson Sá: Art Director
Brian Garvey: Designer
Cindy Reiman: Photography Manager

Library of Congress Cataloging-in-Publication Data

Staley, Erin, author.
Discovering ancient Egypt/Erin Staley.—First edition.
     pages cm.—(Exploring ancient civilizations)
ISBN 978-1-62275-830-2 (library bound)—ISBN 978-1-62275-829-6 (pbk.)—
ISBN 978-1-62275-828-9 (6-pack)
1. Egypt—Civilization—To 332 B.C—Juvenile literature. 2. Egypt—Civilization—332 B.C.-638 A.D.—Juvenile literature. 3. Egypt—Antiquities—Juvenile literature. I. Title. II. Series: Exploring ancient civilizations.
DT61.S858 2014
932.01—dc23

                                                                        2014025955

Manufactured in the United States of America

Photo credits: Cover, pp. 1, 3 Dudarev Mikhail/Shutterstock.com; p. 7 Sophie McAulay/Shutterstock.com; p. 9 © nicolas lecoz/Fotolia; p. 10 Bob Burch/Bruce Coleman Inc.; pp. 12, 18 DEA/G. Dagli Orti/De Agostini/Getty Images; pp. 13, 16 Hirmer Fotoarchiv, Munich; p. 17 Print Collector/Hulton Archive/Getty Images; p. 21 © uwimages/Fotolia; p. 23 © Photos.com/Jupiterimages; p. 25 DEA/W. Buss/De Agostini/Getty Images; p. 26 Top Photo Corporation/Thinkstock; p. 27 moonfish8/Shutterstock.com; p. 28 Private Collection / The Stapleton Collection / Bridgeman Images; p. 31 Encyclopedia Britannica, Inc.; p. 32 Waj/Shutterstock.com; p. 34 A. DEA/A. Dagli Orti/De Agostini/Getty Images; p. 37 Heritage Images/Hulton Archive/Getty Images; p. 40 Zoran Karapancev/Shutterstock.com; p. 41 Universal Images Group/Getty Images; p. 42 Philippe Huguen/AFP/Getty Images; cover and interior graphics © iStockphoto.com/ksana-gribakina (patterned banners and borders), HorenkO/Shutterstock.com and Freckles/Shutterstock.com (background textures).

CONTENTS

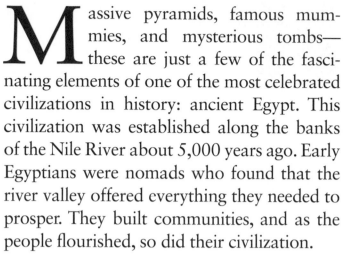

Massive pyramids, famous mummies, and mysterious tombs—these are just a few of the fascinating elements of one of the most celebrated civilizations in history: ancient Egypt. This civilization was established along the banks of the Nile River about 5,000 years ago. Early Egyptians were nomads who found that the river valley offered everything they needed to prosper. They built communities, and as the people flourished, so did their civilization.

From writing to religion, the ancient Egyptians left a legacy for future civilizations to admire and copy. Egypt is credited with making paper; creating the first-known solar calendar; refining scientific, mathematical, and agricultural techniques; developing irrigation systems; and establishing a government that lasted for more than 3,000 years. Ancient Egypt was the superpower of its time. Nonetheless, like other giants of the ancient world, it eventually perished. Climate, corruption, and foreign invaders all played a part in the demise of this notable society. However, ancient Egypt's legacy and achievements continue to capture our imaginations and inspire the arts and sciences to this day.

Carved about 2500 BCE, the Great Sphinx stands before the pyramid complex in Giza, Egypt, and is one of the most recognizable symbols of ancient Egypt. It measures 172 feet (52.4 meters) in length and 66 feet (20 meters) in height.

In what follows, we will explore the early settlement of ancient Egypt. We'll discover how they built their society and set standards in every aspect of civilization. We'll also visit the most exciting moments of Egyptian history and touch on its most famous pharaohs. Finally, we'll look at the immeasurable mark ancient Egypt has left on our culture today.

CHAPTER ONE
SETTLEMENT OF
THE NILE VALLEY

For more than 10,000 years, hunters and gatherers roamed the Nile valley in northeastern Africa. A swampy plateau overgrown with trees, rushes, and papyrus, the narrow valley was home to the world's longest river, the Nile. As the climate became hot and dry, harsh desert conditions developed on either side of the 4,132-mile-long (6,650 kilometer) river. The Nile became the only oasis for drinking water, food, and transportation. Eventually it became what the ancient Egyptians believed to be the gateway to the afterlife.

This dependency on the Nile, both physical and spiritual, is reflected in the first verses of the ancient "Hymn to the Nile": "Hail to thee, O Nile! Who manifests thyself over this land, and comes to give life to Egypt!" The formerly nomadic Egyptians established villages and towns along its riverbanks. The time of this settlement is known as the Predynastic

Known for being the longest river in the world, the Nile rises just south of the equator and flows northward through northeastern Africa. Its waters drain into the Mediterranean Sea.

Era (5th millennium BCE–c. 2925 BCE). It would be the origins of one of antiquity's most important civilizations: ancient Egypt.

Agriculture and Dietary Habits

In order to control the Nile, the ancient Egyptians invented a year-round irrigation system. It sent river water along short canals to nearby fields. With an ongoing watering system, farmers could plant seeds and grains. They developed a measuring system that allowed them to plant such crops as wheat

About 96 percent of Egypt's total area is desert. To aid in the cultivation of produce, farmers use irrigation on the banks of the Nile River. This practice — which is still used today — dates back to ancient times.

and barley. These ingredients were used to make such Egyptian staples as bread, soup, and beer. The ancient Egyptians also used the land to domesticate long-horned cattle, sheep, goats, and geese. These animals provided food, and the cattle also supplied labor to plow the fields and carry heavy loads.

Ancient Egyptian Artisans

The ancient Egyptians were skilled artisans. They used nearby resources to build homes,

CIVILIZATION'S FIRST SOLAR CALENDAR

Egyptian farmers set out to predict the Nile's flooding cycle. They wanted to determine when the ideal planting season would come each year. In approximately 4236 BCE, they created a 365-day agricultural calendar. This was the first solar calendar consisting of 365 days in recorded history. The Egyptian calendar consisted of 12 months. Each month was made up of 30 days. An additional five days were added at the end of each year to keep calendar dates better aligned with the sun's movement. The calendar year was divided into three seasons: the inundation (flooding season), winter (when the waters receded), and summer (the dry season or harvest). The agricultural calendar made it possible for farmers to harvest a high yield of annual crops.

make clothing, and craft home goods. The first Egyptian homes were lightly built huts. However, later homes were made of mud bricks and more sophisticated. They had wood-framed doors, small windows, and floors of straw matting. Paintings often decorated the walls, and although wood was scarce, it was eventually imported

Much of what we know today about ancient Egyptian artistry comes from the rich findings that archaeologists have made. This painted jar—made sometime between 1200 and 1050 BCE—demonstrates the style of artisan crafts created during the New Kingdom.

from other lands to make furniture.

Egyptian artisans also sculpted clay for pottery. They carved ivory for ornaments and cut stone for religious figurines. They spun and wove flax for white linen clothing. This style of dress helped them keep cool in the scorching climate. Men wore skirts, and women wore straight, ankle-length dresses. Paperworkers gathered papyrus reeds from the Nile marshes to make pale-yellow writing paper. Weavers used the reeds for baskets, mats, rope, and sandals. Metalworkers used metals and precious stones to fashion jewelry, dishes, tools, and weapons.

Significantly, boat makers built vessels to sail and trade with foreign lands. These vessels were "signed" for identification, a signature later believed by Egyptologists—those who study Egypt—to be among the first acts of writing. In fact, many of ancient Egypt's artisan goods were preserved over generations and discovered by archaeologists. Today they give us great insight into the resources and lifestyle of the ancient Egyptians.

Two Kingdoms

As a reliable food supply increased, so did the population. All Egyptians contributed

A temple carving made during the 12th dynasty (about 1756 BCE) depicts the crown of Lower Egypt on the left and the crown of Upper Egypt on the right.

to the development of their society. Political leaders planned the workload and directed the artisan and farmer workforces. In time, small settlements grew into larger communities. These communities organized themselves into two kingdoms. Upper Egypt was in the narrow river valley in the south. Lower Egypt was in the north, in the broad delta (triangular piece of land) where the river flows into the Mediterranean Sea.

Each kingdom had its own capital city and king. Upper and Lower Egypt traded crops, goods, and cattle with other communities along the Nile. With plenty of food, a successful government structure, and natural barriers to help protect them from enemies—the sea to the north and deserts to the east and west—Egypt was free to establish its civilization. Its people explored new interests, such as the arts, religion, language, and science. This exploration helped them build the legacy of ancient Egypt.

CHAPTER TWO

FEATURES OF AN ANCIENT CIVILIZATION

With the settlement of hunter-gatherers along the Nile valley came the emergence of ancient Egyptian society. This society developed a class system, religious beliefs, a writing system, and masterful artwork. The Egyptians' greatest creative period was early in their long history. After that, their way of living changed very little through the many years and kingdoms. It is therefore possible to describe much of their culture without reference to the historical periods of Egyptian history.

The Class System of Ancient Egypt

The growth of ancient Egyptian society in its early period led to a formalized class system. This class system gave different groups of Egyptians specific jobs. At the top of the social order was the pharaoh, or

This sandstone pillar statue (c. 1370 BCE) depicts Akhenaton, king of Egypt from 1353–36 BCE. Pharaohs in ancient Egypt stood at the top of the social hierarchy and were greatly revered.

king. Egyptians respected their pharaohs greatly and even worshiped them at certain points in history.

Pharaohs relied on a class of nobles for administrative purposes. These high-ranking officials held government posts and were paid handsomely from tributes offered to the pharaoh. They organized local militias—the soldiers of ancient Egypt. Pharaohs also relied on scribes. These scholars were responsible for writing administrative and religious records.

The luxurious life of the upper classes was made possible by the continual labor of the peasants who tilled the soil. Also ranking below the nobles (although with much easier lives than the peasants) were Egypt's craftsmen and artists. Their jobs were inherited, passed from father to son. Through their efforts, ancient Egypt developed advanced crafts and left a rich array of cultural relics.

Although slavery was not common in ancient Egypt, some people were kept as slaves. These slaves were generally foreigners—non-Egyptians taken captive in war or traded to the Egyptians. However, some Egyptians were forced by poverty or debt to sell themselves into service. Some slaves served in the homes of the nobility. Others—mostly prisoners of war—were forced to work in the fields, in the mines, or in military engagements.

Religious Beliefs

A pluralistic religion—the belief in multiple deities—was the glue of ancient Egyptian society. This ancient Egyptian religion was very complex. Its most striking feature was the vast number of gods and goddesses who could be depicted in human, animal, or other forms. The gods were never grouped sys-tematically, and many of them were interchangeable.

Wall paintings often depicted the lives of the different social classes in ancient Egypt. Shown here is a wall painting from an artisan's tomb at Saqqara. In addition to the workers, note the record-keeping scribes on the bottom right.

A painted wooden ceremonial slab (Third Intermediate Period, 12th dynasty) depicts rays emitting from Re, the sun god, in the shape of lotus flowers. Re was one of the central gods in ancient Egyptian religious beliefs.

Since they had different forms, the gods also personified different powers. Re was the supreme sun god and father of all creation. Re encompassed numerous attributes and was often merged with other gods to form composite gods. Pharaohs claimed their legitimacy to the throne as descendants of Re.

Another central Egyptian god was Amon. When the city of Thebes became the capital of Egypt (around 2050 BCE), Amon became the god of the Egyptian empire. Amon's name meant "the hidden one." He became the greatest god in Egyptian mythology and

GODS AND GODDESSES OF ANCIENT EGYPT

Egyptians prayed to the different gods based on their powers. The following are a few more of the most important Egyptian gods:

ANUBIS God of the dead, represented by a jackal or the figure of a man with the head of a jackal.

BASTET A cat-headed goddess associated with music and dancing and with protection against diseases and evil spirits.

HORUS Hawk- or falcon-headed sky god.

ISIS and **OSIRIS** Iris was the queen of the gods, while her brother and husband, Osiris, was a fertility god, giver of civilization, and ruler of the dead. Horus was their son.

MAAT Goddess of law, justice, and truth.

PTAH God of the arts, crafts, and trades.

SEKHMET The lion-headed war goddess.

THOTH Ibis-headed god of wisdom, intelligence, and magic.

was linked with Re. His name then became Amon-Re.

Religion was upheld by the priesthood. They preserved ancient Egyptian culture, traditions, and social hierarchy. Priests acted as political advisors to the pharaohs.

They studied the movements of the planets and stars, recited prayers, oversaw funerals, and carried offerings for the dead.

Tombs and Mummies

Ancient Egyptian tombs were designed to help the dead navigate their way to the afterlife. Egyptians buried mummies in these chambers, which were sometimes located in or under pyramids. Salt and chemicals were used to preserve the corpses of royals and nobles as mummies. The bodies were then laid in fancy coffins called sarcophagi. Ancient Egyptians also made mummies of such sacred animals as cats, ibises, and crocodiles.

Wealthy Egyptian families stocked their tombs with items that they thought would be of use in the next life, including tools, figurines, and weaponry. The massive tombs were also carved with pictures, paintings, and inscriptions.

Hieroglyphics

One of ancient Egypt's finest achievements was hieroglyphics. This name (which means "sacred carving") was given by the Greeks to the Egyptian system of pictures cut or painted onto tomb and temple walls. Egyptians began using hieroglyphics by 3100 BCE. Originally, they were written in vertical columns. Later they were written in horizontal rows from right to left.

Each hieroglyph represented the sound of the names of the object pictured. For example, the hieroglyph for "house" had two purposes: it meant "house" and also

Hieroglyphics adorn a temple wall at Karnak, Egypt. Hieroglyphics are pictures as well as signs with a sound value. They were the building blocks of the ancient Egyptian language.

stood for the sound of the Egyptian word for house, *pr*. The symbol looked like this:

Eventually, the ancient Egyptians developed two simpler forms of writing similar to modern-day cursive: hieratic for religious texts and demotic for political or administrative documents. The discovery in 1799 of the Rosetta Stone—an irregularly shaped stone featuring ancient Greek, demotic, and hieroglyphic writing—helped linguists decode hieroglyphics.

Ancient Egyptian Art

Ancient Egypt's paintings and sculptures were masterpieces of their time. Artists illustrated the ideal relationship between deities, rulers, and mankind. They ignored realistic perspective in order to depict religious and social standards. For example, the bodies of pharaohs and nobles were painted larger than those of the working class. Heads were in profile while bodies were in frontal view. If the pharaohs were old or injured, they were made to look youthful and healthy. This translated over to the thousands of sculptures that were created depicting favored deities and leaders. Pharaohs were often depicted in half-human, half-animal forms. They were always shown in static, larger-than-life poses.

In general, ancient Egypt's art changed very little over the course of its 3,000-year existence. However, small style changes did occur when new rulers took the throne. As foreign invaders took over, their styles, races, and cultures also influenced Egyptian art. In the Greco-Roman period, art in Alexandria mirrored Greek influences.

The Rosetta Stone (196 BCE) was fashioned from volcanic rock in Rosetta (Rashid), Egypt. Its discovery in 1799 helped modern linguists decipher hieroglyphics. Today the stone is on display in the British Museum in London, United Kingdom.

CHAPTER THREE
EGYPT'S OLD AND MIDDLE KINGDOMS

Around 3100 BCE the powerful king of Upper Egypt, Menes, conquered Lower Egypt, uniting the two kingdoms into the Kingdom of Two Lands. Menes established a new capital in the city of Memphis, where Upper and Lower Egypt met on the west bank of the Nile.

After Menes, many pharaohs ruled ancient Egypt. During the long history of the Egyptian civilization, there were more than 30 dynasties, or ruling families, of pharaohs. Modern historians have grouped several of these dynasties into three important periods: the Old Kingdom, the Middle Kingdom, and the New Kingdom. The first two of these flourishing times are discussed in this chapter.

The Old Kingdom

Throughout the Old Kingdom (c. 2575–c. 2130 BCE), ancient Egypt thrived. Although the first pyramids had been built by this time—most notably the architect Imhotep's Step Pyramid at Ṣaqqārah for King Djoser—it was during the Old Kingdom that the greatest of pyramids were constructed.

The climax of pyramid building was reached in the three enormous tombs erected for the kings Khufu, Khafre, and Menkaure at Giza. Each pyramid guarded the body of one king, housed in a chamber deep within the structure. To the south of the Great Pyramid lies the Great Sphinx, the best known of all Egyptian sculpture. Carved out of limestone, the Great Sphinx has human facial features but the body of a lion. The head is believed to be

King Djoser's Step Pyramid (Old Kingdom, 3rd dynasty) in the Saqqara Necropolis, Memphis, Egypt, was the first of its kind. It paved the way for the smoother, sloping-sided pyramids of later kingdoms.

To the left of the Great Sphinx is the Pyramid of Menkaure. It was the last to be constructed of the three major pyramids at Giza. Its completed height is 218 feet (66 meters).

a portrait of Khafre. In ancient times the pyramids of Giza were included among the Seven Wonders of the World. Today they are the only one of those wonders that still exists.

Eventually, the climate in Egypt became drier. A series of droughts and famines hastened the fall of the Old Kingdom, and a period of decline known as the First Intermediate Period (c. 2130–1938 BCE) followed. It was a dark time, as Egypt suffered civil wars. Noblemen abused power;

warlords fought among themselves; thieves stole from the pyramids; and ancient Egypt was again divided.

The Middle Kingdom

Egypt reunited during the Middle Kingdom (1938–c. 1630 BCE). The pharaohs strengthened the military, warding off enemies and claiming more territory. The arts and sciences flourished once again, and the Temple of Amon at Karnak— one of the period's most significant structures—was built to commemorate Egypt's unification and spirituality.

During the Middle Kingdom, the Egyptians used their resources more efficiently. Massive irrigation systems were assembled in Al-Fayyum. Pharaohs were buried inside hidden tombs rather than inside expensive

The Great Temple of Amon at Karnak is a massive temple complex with no fewer than 10 pylons—massive stone structures that flanked the doors to temples. Carved with decorations, these pylons formed gateways that linked the temple to other temples nearby.

THE HYKSOS

Robert Ambrose Dudley's *The Expulsion of the Hyksos* lithograph (c. 1910) shows the Egyptian army following the Hyksos as they cross northern Sinai into southern Canaan (modern Israel).

The Hyksos were foreign rulers who invaded Egypt and used their military advancements to claim Egyptian land. Their chariots, horses, compound bows, superior battle axes, and defensive techniques were too much for the Egyptians, who had to fight them on foot. Learning from the Hyksos, the Egyptians began practicing new warfare methods. Hyksos rule advanced Egypt and set it up for its next period of success.

pyramids. Trade picked up again as ships were sent across the Mediterranean Sea to foreign lands. The Egyptians imported copper and turquoise from Sinai mines and gold and semiprecious stones from Nubia, as well as ivory, ebony, incenses, animal skins, ostrich feathers, and live animals. Slaves from Nubia were traded for luxury goods and food.

Commercialism allowed a middle class to develop. Individuals realized their personal rights. They began participating in burial practices once limited to royalty. The funerary god Osiris became available to everyone for worship. Peace and prosperity prevailed for more than two centuries until the Egyptians lost—for the first time—to their longtime enemies, the Hyksos.

By 1539 BCE, King Ahmose I of Lower Egypt had forced the Hyksos out. Upper and Lower Egypt were unified again, and Ahmose became the pharaoh of a united Egypt. Having destroyed the Hyksos stronghold at Avaris, in the eastern Nile delta, Ahmose eventually drove the Hyksos beyond the eastern Egyptian frontier and then invaded southern Palestine; the full extent of his conquests may have been much greater. Ahmose's success came at a time when there was no other major established power in the Middle East. This political gap set the stage for the creation of an Egyptian empire.

CHAPTER FOUR

THE AGE OF EMPIRE: THE NEW KINGDOM

The New Kingdom period (1540–1075 BCE) was Egypt's age of empire, during which the once-peaceful Egyptians embarked on foreign conquest on a large scale. Under a series of ambitious rulers, Egyptian borders stretched from Syria to the Sudan. Diplomacy was established with foreign countries, and slaves and tributes poured in from conquered nations.

Hatshepsut and Thutmose III

Egypt's first great female leader, Hatshepsut, came to power during the 18th dynasty. When her husband, Thutmose II, died about 1479 BCE, the throne passed to his son Thutmose III. As Thutmose III was still an infant, Hatshepsut at first acted as regent for the young king. Later, she and Thutmose III were corulers of Egypt, with Hatshepsut very much the dominant leader. During her reign, Hatshepsut commissioned the now-famous pillar-shaped monuments called obelisks.

Following Hatshepsut's death in about 1458 BCE, Thutmose III took over in his own right. He was a skilled general who led many successful military campaigns that established Egyptian supremacy in parts of Syria and western Asia.

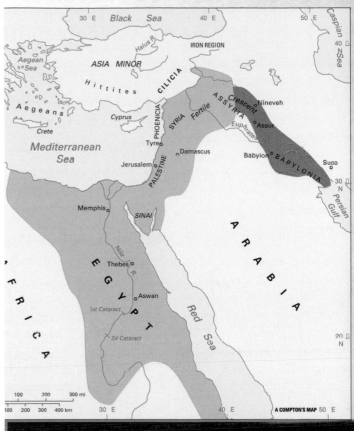

This map shows the far-reaching stretch of the ancient Egyptian empire at the time of Thutmose III's death in 1426 BCE.

Upon his death, Egypt controlled Nubia, parts of Canaan (modern-day Israel), and the coasts of Syria and Lebanon. Thutmose's reign marked the height of ancient Egypt's power and wealth.

Amenhotep III and Akhenaton

Thutmose IV's son Amenhotep III, who ruled from 1390 to 1353 BCE, built the magnificent Temple of Luxor in Thebes and ordered the construction of the colossal seated statues called the Colossi of Memnon. Both demonstrated the ultimate in royal opulence. In the last years of his reign Amenhotep III paid little attention to the empire. It was already decaying when his son Amenhotep IV came to the

The two great statues known as the Colossi of Memnon once flanked the gateway in front of the Temple of Luxor. The carved quartzite blocks stand at 75 feet (23 meters) and weigh more than 1,000 tons (907 metric tons).

throne in 1353 BCE. Amenhotep IV was more interested in religion than in warfare. Even before his father's death, he began to promote a new religious doctrine. He wanted the people to abandon their old gods and worship only one sun god of his preference, Aton.

Amenhotep IV changed his name to Akhenaton, a name meaning "beneficial to the Aton," and he moved the capital of Egypt to a new site called Akhetaton. He married Nefertiti, a woman known for her great beauty. She frequently made offerings to Aton even though it was a religious rite reserved for male rulers. Akhenaton's successor, King Tutankhamen, who took the throne in 1333 BCE when he was only about nine years old and who ruled until his death in 1323 BCE, restored the traditional Egyptian religion. During his short reign, he also returned the capital to Thebes. King Tutankhamen is famous for his extravagantly furnished tomb, which was discovered intact in the Valley of the Kings in 1922.

Ramses II and Ramses III

Ramses II came to power in 1279 BCE and reigned for more than 60 years. He quelled rebellions in southern Syria and fought the Hittites at the Battle of Kadesh. He captured towns in Galilee and Amor, but, unable to defeat the Hittites, he agreed to a peace treaty in 1258 BCE. He married one and perhaps two of the Hittite king's daughters, and the later part of his reign was free from war. Its prosperity may be measured by the amount of construction he undertook. Early on he built a city in the Nile delta as a base for military campaigns and resumed construction of the temple of Osiris, begun by his father, Seti I. He added to the temple at Karnak and completed a temple for his father at Luxor. For his wife, Nefertari, he had two mountains crafted into temples at Abu Simbel. One was dedicated to her and the other to himself. Today these monuments still stand near the present-day border between Egypt and Sudan.

Ramses III (ruled 1187–1156 BCE) is

Ramses II is known for a series of decisive military victories early in his reign. In this New Kingdom–era painting he is pictured holding a group of prisoners by their hair. Today the painting is on display at the Egyptian Museum in Cairo, Egypt.

34

THE FIRST RECORDED LABOR STRIKE

As grand as the New Kingdom was, it was what began the downturn of ancient Egypt. Wartime and extensive construction projects put a significant drain on the treasury. During the final years of Ramses III's rule, the government had been troubled with administrative difficulties, conspiracies, and corruption. The government could no longer pay elite craftsmen.

Hungry and unpaid, workers employed on the royal tombs at Thebes went on strike. It was the first recorded labor strike in history. Desperate, they tunneled into hidden tombs for precious stones, jewelry, gold, and silver. Eventually, the Upper Egypt vizier stepped in. He assumed responsibility for all of Egypt and put an end to the strike.

believed to be the last great ancient Egyptian king. He enjoyed military victory against foreign invaders in three great wars. Because of these victories, tranquility prevailed during much of Ramses III's reign.

During the Third Intermediate Period (1075–656 BCE), Theban priests gained control of much of the southern Nile River valley while foreign rulers controlled territory elsewhere. During the Late Period (664–332 BCE), Egypt's power continued to wane. Persia conquered Egypt from 525 BCE until 404 BCE. Three brief Egyptian dynasties followed, the last of which fell to a second Persian conquest in 341 BCE.

The Greco-Roman Period

Persian rule lasted until the Macedonian conqueror Alexander the Great invaded Egypt in 332 BCE. He established the capital city of Alexandria. After Alexander's death, Ptolemy, one of his generals, assumed leadership of the empire. A new dynasty known as the Ptolemies began. The Ptolemies were Macedonians who spoke Greek. They introduced Greek manners and ideas into Egyptian culture.

The Ptolemies left their mark in part by building a massive lighthouse, the Pharos of Alexandria. It was considered one of the Seven Wonders of the World while it stood. The Ptolemies also built the famous Library at Alexandria—the greatest collection of classical writings in the ancient world. Neither of these Ptolemaic contributions stands today. The Ptolemaic dynasty ended with Queen Cleopatra, the most famous female ruler of the ancient world.

Queen Cleopatra

Cleopatra was born in Alexandria in 69 BCE. Cleopatra came to the throne as coruler with her brother, Ptolemy XIII, in 51 BCE. Soon, however, her brother's supporters drove the queen from power. She turned to the power-ful Roman ruler Julius Caesar. Caesar was charmed by Cleopatra and helped her regain the throne. Cleopatra bore Caesar a son,

Maarten van Heemskerck's illustration of the Pharos of Alexandria (1572) depicts the famous Ptolemaic period lighthouse that once stood on the Egyptian coast. The massive lighthouse was a technological triumph and is the archetype of all light-houses since.

Caesarion. The three lived in Rome until Caesar's assassination in 44 BCE. After the deaths of both Ptolemy XIII and his suc-cessor, Ptolemy XIV, Cleopatra named her infant son coruler.

Desiring increased power, Cleopatra turned to Mark Antony, controller of

Rome's eastern territories. Antony, like Caesar, was charmed by the queen. Although he was already married, Antony had twins by Cleopatra. When his wife died, Antony returned to Rome, where he was forced to marry Octavia, sister of the powerful Octavian (later Emperor Augustus). Eventually, however, Antony returned to Alexandria to reunite with Cleopatra. This angered Octavian, who declared war against the two lovers. He defeated them in several key battles. Antony killed himself and, according to legend, Cleopatra likewise committed suicide by letting an asp, a symbol of divine royalty, bite her.

After Cleopatra's death in 30 BCE, Egypt was proclaimed a province of Rome. The Romans held Egypt from 30 BCE to 395 CE; later it was part of the Byzantine Empire. Egypt eventually came under Arab control in 642.

CHAPTER FIVE
THE LEGACY OF ANCIENT EGYPT

Powerful and sophisticated, ancient Egypt's culture greatly influenced other civilizations. The Assyrians, Persians, Greeks, and Romans all tried to match the magnificence of this superpower. From art and architecture to science and religion, ancient Egypt stood out in the Mediterranean world with its great advances, and it continues to influence our own civilization, thousands of years later.

Egypt Inspires Future Civilizations

Though many of the stories of ancient Egypt were preserved on papyrus documents and inscribed on monuments, they went undeciphered for centuries. The decoding of hieroglyphics in the 19th century helped rescue them. Finally, many of the keys to understanding ancient Egyptian civilization were revealed

The Louvre Museum in Paris, France, is host to one of the richest art collections in the world. Its modern entrance, a steel-and-glass pyramid designed by the American architect I. M. Pei, is a contemporary nod to ancient Egyptian architecture.

to the world. We now know a great deal about the Egyptians' history and culture.

As ancient Egypt phased out of existence, its deities and beliefs in an afterlife continued to have fans in Rome and Greece. Many scholars believe that elements of Egyptian spirituality influenced other great religions, including Judaism and Christianity. Egypt's pyramids and temples inspired centuries of artists, architects, writers, and explorers. The pyramid form came to play an important role in modern architecture. Some famous examples of Egyptian-inspired structures include the Pyramid Arena in Memphis, Tennessee, the Louvre Pyramid in Paris, France, and the Palace of Peace and Reconciliation in Astana, Kazakhstan. Egyptian pyramids also testify to the advanced mathematical skills that were used. Without calculators and computers, ancient Egyptians were able

CLEOPATRA'S LEGACY

Cleopatra's history is forever intertwined with that of Egypt and Rome, and her dramatic story has been immortalized in retellings and reinterpretations through the ages. In Western culture, she's been depicted as a temptress. In Muslim scholarship, she was shown as a scholar, philosopher, scientist, and chemist. The great English poet and playwright William Shakespeare used Greek biographer Plutarch's *Parallel Lives* to pen *Antony and Cleopatra* (1606). There she was portrayed as a heroine. Other artists used this as material for Cleopatra-themed works of literature and visual and performance art. Hollywood even told romanticized stories of a seductive and ambitious Cleopatra on the silver screen. Perhaps the most famous is actress Elizabeth Taylor's portrayal of the queen in *Cleopatra*, filmed in 1963.

This illustration by 19th-century English painter Frederick Sandys (1866) shows Cleopatra, whose seductive beauty has made her an attractive figure in the arts and popular culture into modern times.

to design and build these monuments with awe-inspiring precision.

Ancient Egyptians also developed highly advanced medical skills. Greek and Roman physicians learned from Egyptian dissection and mummification techniques. Today the medical community still looks to ancient Egypt for answers. Studies of the preservation of mummies have revealed some of the illnesses suffered at that time, including arthritis, tuberculosis of the bone, gout, tooth decay, bladder stones, and gallstones;

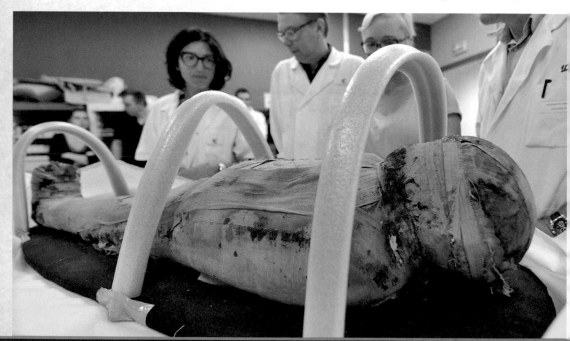

Egyptian mummies have proven to be an important resource for modern researchers in a variety of fields. Some radiologists, forensic scientists, natural historians, and anatomy researchers have used mummies to study the diseases that afflicted ancient Egyptians. Some hope to stop those very diseases today.

there is evidence, too, of the parasitic disease schistosomiasis, or bilharzia, which still affects at least 200 million people yearly in Africa, Asia, and elsewhere and which remains prevalent in the Nile valley. If left untreated, schistosomiasis can lead to bladder cancer. Scientists hope that by studying the impact of schistosomiasis on ancient populations, they may better understand how to control this and other parasitic diseases that continue to plague people today.

Conclusion

Thousands of years later, Egypt continues to pique our curiosity. Egypt's place is secured: with courses in Egyptology, books, TV programs, museum exhibits, and Hollywood films, ancient Egypt's prominent place in our culture is evident. Despite all that we know about the civilization, many questions about the lives and culture of the ancient Egyptians remain. This lack of certainty adds to the appeal, inspiring historians, archaeologists, and other researchers to discover more. Who knows which mysteries of this most celebrated ancient civilization will be revealed next?

GLOSSARY

ANTIQUITY Ancient times, especially those before the Middle Ages.

ARCHAEOLOGIST A scientist who studies past human life as shown by fossil relics and the monuments and tools left by ancient peoples.

DEITY Supernatural being, such as any of the ancient Egyptian gods and goddesses.

DELTA The triangular or fan-shaped piece of land made by deposits of mud and sand at the mouth of a river.

DIPLOMACY The act of managing relationships among foreign nations.

DYNASTY A period of rule in which all leaders come from the same family.

EGYPTOLOGY The study of ancient Egypt, spanning the period c. 4500 BCE to 641 CE.

HITTITES Members of a conquering people in Asia Minor and Syria with an empire in the 2nd millennium BCE.

OASIS A fertile or green spot in a desert.

PAPYRUS Thick paper-like material made from large papyrus reeds that grew along the Nile River.

PLATEAU A broad, flat area of high level ground.

PREDYNASTIC Also known as prehistoric, the Predynastic Period is specific to ancient Egypt's time period before dynasties existed.

REGENT A person who governs a kingdom when a monarch is not able to.

RUSH Any of various marsh plants that are monocotyledons, often having hollow stems and sometimes used to weave chair seats and mats.

SARCOPHAGUS Stone coffin whose use dates back to the Egyptian 3rd dynasty.

STRIKE An organized effort by workers who stop working with the intention of forcing an employer to meet their demands.

TRIBUTE Something (as a gift or speech of praise) that is given or performed to show appreciation, respect, or affection.

VIZIER The second in command to the pharaoh.

Boyer, Crispin. *Everything Ancient Egypt* (National Geographic Kids). Des Moines, IA: National Geographic Children's Books, 2012.

Fleming, Fergus. *Ancient Egypt's Myths and Beliefs.* New York, NY: Rosen Publishing, 2012.

Green, Roger Lancelyn. *Tales of Ancient Egypt.* New York, NY: The Penguin Group, 2008.

Hart, George. *DK Eyewitness Books: Ancient Egypt.* New York, NY: Dorling Kindersley Limited, 2008.

Robins, Gay. *The Art of Ancient Egypt: Revised Edition.* Cambridge, MA: Harvard University Press, 2008.

Rockwood, Leigh. *Ancient Egyptian Economy.* New York, NY: Rosen Publishing, 2014.

Rockwood, Leigh. *Ancient Egyptian Geography.* New York, NY: Rosen Publishing, 2014.

Smith, Miranda. *Navigators: Ancient Egypt.* New York, NY: Kingfisher, 2010.

Steele, Philip. *Ancient Egypt.* New York, NY: Rosen Publishing, 2009.

Websites

Because of the changing nature of Internet links, Rosen Publishing has developed an online list of websites related to the subject of this book. This site is updated regularly. Please use this link to access this list:

http://www.rosenlinks.com/ANCIV/Egypt

INDEX

11/16